ALL ABOUT THE MIRACLES

And Other Contemplations on God's Holy Word

A Book of Poems
BY MAYNA COSBY

All About the Miracles ... And Other Contemplations on God's Holy Word

Copyright 2020 Mayna Cosby

All Rights Reserved

ISBN 978-1-940645-83-4

Greenville, South Carolina

PUBLISHED IN THE UNITED STATES OF AMERICA

Dedication

I dedicate this simple book of poems to those who love our Lord Jesus Christ and to those who are sincerely searching.

"I love those who love Me, and those who seek Me diligently will find Me." (Proverbs 8:17)

Foreword

This small book on the miracles of Jesus is not so much a focus on the miracles themselves, but on the one who performed them.

We look with amazement into that magnanimous heart of Jesus — and are awed by His radical love, depth of compassion, and His forgiveness unto salvation.

I am thankful for the writings of Matthew Henry, John MacArthur and John R. Rice, who continue to inspire me.

Mayna Cosby
July 2020

"When I have asked the reader to look into his heart,
I have done so and have found myself wanting."

Table of Contents

The Miracles

- Zacchaeus 13
- Jesus Turns Water into Wine 16
- A Child's Demon Cast Out 18
- Jesus Heals a Sick Man 21
- A Widow's Miracle 24
- A Nobleman's Son Healed 27
- The Widow of Zarephath 29
- Blind Bartimaeus 32
- Jesus Quells the Storm 35
- Jesus Heals a Woman 37
- Nicodemus 39
- Jesus Cures a Paralyzed Servant 41
- Jesus Walks on Water 43
- The Canaanite Woman 46
- Jesus Ousts an Evil Spirit 49
- The Ten Lepers 51
- The Memorial Gift 52
- Jesus Heals Blind Eyes 54
- Who Is My Neighbor? 59
- Jesus Heals a Shriveled Hand 62
- Jarius' Daughter Raised 64
- The Crown of Thorns 67
- Jesus Amazes the Scholars 69
- Jesus Heals a Leper 71

Other Contemplations

- The Rose of Sharon 75
- Rachel and Leah 77
- A Greater Thing 81
- David and Abigail 82
- Prayer/Thoughts for Israel 86

Plan of Salvation: How to Become a Christian 91

ALL ABOUT THE MIRACLES

And Other Contemplations on God's Holy Word

The Miracles

Zacchaeus

Zacchaeus, Zacchaeus, oh what a reputation!
Only Jesus could bring consolation,
To a name so drenched in forward fame,
To a name so drowned in scandalous shame.

A little man, dark-eyed and cunning,
Traitor to his Jewish birth, how stunning!
No longer a son of Abraham,
More a fox and not a lamb.

Chief of tax collectors, chief of sinners,
Loveless and lost, as cold as the winters.
The people despised him and were quite numb
To what Zacchaeus might one day become.

Of the choicest morsels he did partake,
Dressed in the finest for vanity's sake.
Though nimble and quick in body and mind,
Yet plainly withering on the vine.

Zacchaeus, a mind and heart full of greed,
Oblivious to his prodigious need.
Lacking compassion, humility and mirth,
He had never heard of the second birth.

On his little finger, a ring he wore
And often thought that he was more
Than the common man who passed him by,
And heard not their need or painful cry.

Yet humbling his dignity, he climbed the fig tree,
Jesus! A sudden gripping urge to see!
Then Zacchaeus heard the most compelling sound;
It was Jesus calling Zacchaeus down!

"Zacchaeus, come down now.
I must stay at your house today."
So Zacchaeus immediately shimmied down
And felt a strange excitement round.

The brightness of Jesus' glory burst forth from His eyes;
In himself, Zacchaeus saw the arrogance, the greed, the pride.
His surprised self-recognition broke Zacchaeus' heart
As Jesus dropped the saving seed into the broken part.

Then Zacchaeus dared to gaze deep into Jesus' soul,
Saw the oceans of love more precious than his hoarded gold.
His spirit blossomed like a white, twining rose,
A new and joyful man from his head down to his toes.

The righteous ones were aghast and grumbled
Not seeing that Zacchaeus was so beautifully humbled.
Blind to a pagan becoming a lamb
And now a true son of Abraham!

"Lord, Lord! Here and now I give
Half of my possessions to the poor;
And if I have cheated anybody out of anything,
I will pay back four times the amount!"

Because Jesus had saved him from out of the pit,
The name he had now undeniably fit.
All Zacchaeus' sins, through Jesus, were wondrously undone;
Zacchaeus, his name and person now matching, means: "The just one."

Zacchaeus, Zacchaeus, oh what a name!

(Luke 19:1-10)

Jesus Turns Water into Wine

The third day, Jesus came to Cana of Galilee,
Performed a miracle also for you and me.
The occasion was a marriage, a time for joyful celebration,
As had been throughout the nation for every generation.

For the gloriously, jubilant, happy pair,
They shone like stars free from care.
And the sky graced them with the brightest star,
But God outshone them with *His* Son, by far.

And the luscious food, oh, what a spread!
Just as it should be for those who wed.
And the wine, how generously it flowed
For all those invited to the adorned abode.

Jesus, Mary, and the disciples came;
Jesus, without fame or miracles to His name.
The beautiful festival long continued without fanfare,
Love, affection and fellowship greatly flourished there.

Then, an obstacle rumored, quite contrary,
But believed and acted upon by Mary.
She said to Jesus, "They have no more wine,"
Perhaps expecting from Him a sign.

Jesus asked, "Woman, why do you involve me?"
Calling her woman, showing no partiality.
Jesus lovingly rebuked Mary, for it was not yet His time,
And unknown to Mary, the vats still held some wine.

Delays of mercy are often not denial,
But may seem hard as though a painful trial.
And Mary said to the servants, "Do what He tells you,"
And the servants did just what she said to do.

They filled with water six stone jars to the brim.
Jesus' mother's hope grew perhaps confused or dim.
Then Jesus said, "Take some to the master of the banquet,"
And the servants immediately took it to him.

The master of the banquet was shocked
At how the wine in the water was unlocked.
So thankful that He was saved from embarrassment,
Perhaps from sly remarks or even harassment.

Jesus came to grace and bless them,
And He will meet our need if we let Him.
But if we truly want His care,
We must ask for His presence in daily prayer.

(John 2:1-12)

A Child's Demon Cast Out

When Jesus reached the bottom of the hill,
Many people there were who waited still.
But a poor man knelt down tearfully before Jesus and said,
"Sir, have mercy on my son, for a demon wants him dead!"

"This demon afflicts my child with a life-threatening disorder,
"And violently throws him into the fire and the water.
"And causes him to grind his teeth and his mouth to foam;
"He disappears in an instant and is demon-driven to roam."

His parents gave loving and constant care,
For one of them tried to be always there.
The child's body was covered by sores that bled,
As the evil spirit gleefully wished him dead.

The child could find nothing at all to bring him joy.
Neither gifts nor hope for playing with another little boy.
When his small hand so wanted to grasp a toad or butterfly,
He was thrown violently down, and his wailing parents asked, "Why?"

They listened daily to his blood-curdling cries,
And they watched daily as the light fled from his eyes.
His eyes were nearly stuck together and almost shut.
His nose ran, and flies swarmed about his latest cut.

Satan afflicts the mind that he might taunt the soul,
But these parents were determined, believing and bold.
And though their hearts were rent and shattered,
Help for their son was all that mattered.

The father cried, "Your disciples could not drive the demon out!"
And Jesus answered: "There must not be even a shred of doubt."
For if they had the faith of a tiny mustard seed,
They could ask this mountain to move and it would recede.

Jesus spoke, "Oh, you stubborn, faithless people!
"How long shall I bear with you? Bring him here to me."
Then Jesus rebuked the demon and cast him out,
And those who saw it gave up a mighty shout!

The child's ashen-gray color turned warm,
And his posture took a more upright form.
There was not left one sore or scar.
And his eyes twinkled like the morning star.

He leaped about like a little lamb let out of the foal,
And kissed and hugged his parents with all his soul!
His mother and father, whose lives had been so upended,
Exploded with tears, laughter and joy, their hearts fully mended.

The disciples were embarrassed, but humbled by their plight,
For they had even tried to oust the demon with all their human might.
"But this kind does not go out except by prayer and fasting."
And faith must be mature, strong and lasting.

Are our prayers formal, faithless and weak?
Are our hearts passionate, persistent and meek?
Let us pray fervently and fall down submissively upon our knees,
And know our Lord hears us ...

And in due time will answer all our pleas!

(Matthew 17:14-21, Mark 9:14-27)

Jesus Heals a Sick Man

Up to Jerusalem! Up to the Feast!
All Jewish males from the strong to the weak.
But to the pool of Bethesda Jesus went,
To heal an invalid was His loving intent.

The blind, the lame, the paralyzed, too,
Oh, how pitiful for Gentile and Jew!
Suffering appallingly day after day,
With no caring soul their hope to convey.

An angel stirred the water at times,
But many lay there who were wholly resigned.
For they could not into the water step first,
And felt their lives had been woefully cursed.

Healing came when the water was in motion,
And, oh, how that thought should stir our devotion.
For most of us have blessed good health;
What a godsend it is, much more than wealth!

There lay a man for thirty-eight years,
And God had counted and bottled his tears.
Jesus fastened His eye on the weakest,
The one who had suffered the most and the deepest.

Not the soul's agent but a burden instead,
His poor self lay wasted from his feet to his head.
Sometimes in dreams he saw his body made right,
But his dreams melted like snow in the soft morning light.

"Would you like to get well?" Jesus inquired.
When the water is stirred, I'm too slow and too tired.
"Get up! Pick up your mat and walk," Jesus said.
So he shot to his feet and picked up his bed!

The lame man's body was transformed with health;
Jolted by joy, oh, what emotional wealth!
Muscle and sinew and life in him surged;
Delirious with laughter, his heartache now purged!

The Jews spoke, "It's Sabbath, put down that bed!
It's illegal, you know, but you're ignorant," they said.
It was zeal for the Sabbath the Jews pretended,
Their true desire to kill Jesus, God quickly upended!

And many there were who did not believe,
For a miracle by Jesus they could not conceive.
Evil cannot fathom the beauty of grace,
Just stares at it dumbly with a frown on its face.

Praising God loudly, the man flew to the temple,
Jesus found him and gave a warning so simple:
"Sin no more, for if you do,
Something worse will happen to you!"

The man's infirmity had interrupted his sin,
And that is why Jesus gave a warning to him.
Jesus completed his salvation, body and soul,
The new man stood before Jesus now shining and whole.

We must keep our hearts diligently, open and still;
Be ready and quick to accomplish God's will.
And God should not have to woo or implore us,
To see marvelous miracles dancing right here before us!

(John 5:1-15)

A Widow's Miracle

Near the gate in the small village of Nain,
There trudged an old woman in grievous pain.
Following the bier with the corpse of her son,
A widowed mother, her life hopeless, undone.

Her son, once young and strong, with noble sweetness
That reached out in love, devouring her weakness.
He often brought her lilies that grew by the road,
And his joy and laughter lit up her abode.

Her son, cold-dead now, the image of his father;
Nothing she had asked of him proved a bit of a bother.
He gathered the sticks that kindled the fire,
Baked bread and joyfully did more than required.

Her sweet wrinkled face now so contorted,
All heaven's blessings now wholly aborted.
And her tears flowed like a rushing river down,
Her circumstance, like a heavy chain that bound.

The moon and stars and sun had no shine,
And God had forgotten her as she clung to the vine.
Nothing on earth appealed to her eye,
All strength was gone, now naught but to die.

As the funeral procession moved slowly along,
Her soul was filled with a dirge of wrong.
Many mourners followed expressing great sorrow,
But having little understanding of her fear for tomorrow.

For who would support her when all alone,
And feebleness imprisoned her in breath and bone.
When swindlers swarmed about like flies,
And reduced her to begging with soulful cries.

Then Jesus saw her with tender love,
A depth of feeling that comes from above.
"Don't cry," He said, touching the coffin with command,
And the bearers, by Jesus' wish, halted each man.

"Young man," Jesus said, "come back to life again,"
And the power of love by God's mighty hand
Gave the flame of life to her decaying son,
And Jesus for her a great victory won!

And the young man sat up and began to talk,
So they lowered his stretcher, and he began to walk.
And his mother took him jubilantly into her arms,
Now free from loneliness and other harms.

A mighty prophet has risen among us in Nain,
And he has delivered this widow from an agony of pain.
We have seen the hand of God at work today,
And many praised Him, and some dared to pray.

A report rang out in Judea and across the borders,
Spread among fathers, mothers, sons and daughters,
And we, like this young man, so dead in our sin,
Are, too, given new life, if on Him we depend!

(Luke 7:11-18)

A Nobleman's Son Healed

Jesus again came into Cana of Galilee.
There it was appointed for Him to see
A royal official, whose son lay gravely ill;
And he needed Jesus his hope to fill.

Assaults of pain, of death, and sickness
Fall, too, upon the honorable, only sometimes for wickedness.
The official had such tender affection for his son,
He could have sent a servant, but he himself would come.

Jesus gave a mild rebuke even in the official's grief;
Knowing He would offer soon such grand and sweet relief.
Oh, you who need miracles, signs and wonders to believe,
For your faith so immature it cannot conceive.

If Christ smiles on us, He first frowns,
And if honest, we admit He has many grounds.
Jesus showed him his sin and then for him mercy prepares
And He will do the same for us, for we are beloved heirs.

He begged Jesus to come down before his son died;
It is right to petition, but not to prescribe.
He did not understand that Jesus did not have "to come down,"
For if his son died, Jesus, by natural laws, was never bound.

"You may go, your son will live," Jesus said;
Nothing Jesus spoke or did raised him from his bed.
"Not going down," Jesus did something better and faster,
Proving that truly He was Lord and Master.

The official took Jesus at His word and departed;
No sign or wonder, but he believes and is happy-hearted.
The servants met him with the amazing, awesome news;
There could be no deception, not even the slightest ruse.

For the patient was suddenly healed at the exact seventh hour,
Showing to each one the miracle was by Jesus' mighty power.
Believing in Christ's word, now believing in Christ,
Saved by Him alone, by His coming sacrifice.

The royal official went to Christ alone;
But brought his whole family salvation, joy never known.
Friend, are you experiencing Christ's frown?
Just ask, for His mercy forever abounds.

(John 4:46)

The Widow of Zarephath

Old and forlorn the widow cried
With pent-up pain she could not hide,
And her steps were heavy as her heart
For she and her son, life soon must depart.

All her dreams had vanished or burst;
It seems as though her life were cursed.
A little meal, a little oil,
All that was left of her life of toil.

Her tortured fingers, like the sticks she found,
Were old and gnarled, as she culled the ground.
A little fire she would make;
A little bread she would bake.

Soon in her arms she would mourn her son,
They would eat their last meal, then life would be done.
She would hold him tightly to her breast,
Dying in pain and longing for rest.

Startled, she heard the prophet's cry;
Bring me water and bread that I might not die.
Her eyes were dim and hardly seeing
As she groaned within her spirit being.

Aggrieved, she said, as the Lord your God lives,
I have no loaf but a handful of meal
And a little oil. I'm gathering sticks that I
May bake for me and my son that we may eat bread and then die.

And Elijah answered her: The Lord,
The God of Israel says, "The jar of meal
Shall not waste away, or the bottle of
Oil fail until the day that the Lord sends rain."

Struggling to accept this grand revelation
There fell upon her a heavenly jubilation.
Joyfully she went quickly for the water and bread,
Now so alive when once she was dead!

Her spark of faith brought salvation and grace
And, oh, what a change in her fingers and face!
As the grain and oil multiplied,
Hope for her son and herself was realized.

And the three of them feasted that very night
On fresh bread and olive oil with joy and delight.
And their voices they would often raise,
Giving thanks to God in glorious praise.

And Elijah taught them from the sacred writings
Of Abraham, Moses and the coming good tidings.
And Elijah loved the little fellow
Who often rested upon his pillow.

Life to them now a precious treasure
And God bestowed peace and hope beyond measure.
So the Lord blessed them in all their ways
And Elijah dwelled with them many days.

(1 Kings 17:7-16)

Blind Bartimaeus

A few thought it truly nature's crime
That left the beggar Bartimaeus blind.
Others cared not or said they did not know,
Or blamed him or his parents' sin for his woe.

His eyes, like a dungeon, pitch black as night,
And how often he groaned for the marvel of sight.
As the years passed by, they piled up his grief
But he hung by his fingertips to his hope and belief.

The blush of morning, the sun's pure light,
The shimmering stars that dazzle night,
None of these glories he had ever seen —
But, oh, how his hearing had grown so keen!

And just then Bartimaeus heard a coming crowd,
So he listened intently as it grew ever loud.
And the spirit within him was strangely excited
And his measured hope was clearly ignited.

When he heard that Jesus was passing by,
He knew the Messiah was drawing nigh.
"Jesus, Son of David, have mercy on me."
And his heart prophesied — Jesus, the key!

"Shut up, beggar!" And his hope grew dim.
For why would Jesus want to speak to him?
So deep in distress, Bartimaeus cried all the more,
Louder and louder above the crowd's roar:

"Jesus, Son of David, have mercy on me!"

"Shut up!" The crowd wanted only their voices to raise
And he was interrupting their prattle and praise.
God's law demanded taking care of the needy,
But the leaders and righteous ones were far too greedy.

As Jesus came near, He stopped by the road,
Heard with compassion Bartimaeus' heart-heavy load.
"Tell him to come here," Jesus said to them;
Bartimaeus flung off his old coat and ran stumbling to Him.

"What do you want me to do for you?" Jesus asked.
"O, teacher," the blind man said, "I want to see!"
And Jesus' great power, moved by kindness,
Immediately healed Bartimaeus' blindness.

The dark dungeon burst open
And light, so much brighter than gold,
Blazed miraculously through his being
And lit up his eyes and his soul!

Jesus healed Bartimaeus' eyes and the infection of his soul.
Bartimaeus, now a new man, healthy and whole,
Praising Jesus loudly and going God's way,
Following hard after Jesus — day after day!

(Mark 10:46-52)

Jesus Quells the Storm

Jesus said, "Let us go to the other side."
The disciples with Jesus were happy to oblige.
But they had no vision that their lives someone must save.
If they were not to go down to a watery grave.

Suddenly, as Jesus fell asleep at the stern,
The waters beneath began to swell and churn,
A vicious, dangerous squall was born,
Leaving the disciples frightened and forlorn.

Hugh waves crashed against the distressed vessel,
So severe, no sails or oars could wrestle.
Forgetting that Jesus was by their side,
Their prowess as fishermen melted with their lofty pride.

The angry, swirling winds howled over the stern,
So much so, they feared the boat would overturn.
"Master, Master, don't You care that we drown?"
The disciples were sure the ship was going down!

Jesus slept to test their faith and prayer;
And the sinful disciples thought Jesus did not care.
Against their Lord's kingdom the men committed treason,
For their foolish fear had overwhelmed faith and reason.

Jesus' body slept, but His heart was fully awake,
And His resting body did not His power take.
A tortured ship could never sink,
For Jesus is our saving link.

Jesus' word of command rebuked the storm —
"Quiet! Be still!" the wind and waves collapsed their form.
And as a newborn baby falls asleep,
A blissful peace and hush fell upon the deep.

Jesus reproved the disciples: "Why are you so afraid?"
Where was their foundation Jesus so carefully laid?
And when our sea is tossing, we must "be still!"
For with Jesus at our side, the storm can do no ill.

(Mark 4:35-41)

Jesus Heals a Woman

When Jesus plodded His way through the crowd,
A woman followed with a heart that vowed
To seek out the only one who knew her feeling
And could give her new hope, joy and healing.

She had suffered greatly these many years,
But God had seen and bottled her tears.
Many doctors had treated her blood affliction,
But they treated her mostly without conviction.

She must pay the doctors so her dwelling must be sold
Leaving her penniless and out in the cold.
She felt she was at the end of her rope
And Jesus, she knew, was her last only hope.

She tried so hard to keep herself neat,
And she did quite well, save her locks and her feet.
Her long, tangled hair and her garments so tattered,
But reaching Jesus was all that mattered.

The thought she held now filled her with dread,
To touch Jesus' robe by just one thread.
So she gathered her strength in spite of raw pain
And focused on what she might venture to gain.

She struggled inch by inch, wriggling through the crowd;
The throng pushed and abused her with curses quite loud.
"If I can touch His clothing, I will be healed," she said.
But her strength was all gone, and her feet were like lead.

She prayed a brief prayer, then a sudden jolt
And she surged forward like a lightning bolt!
Her healed body and spirit truly did soar
When she touched the robe that Jesus wore.

"Who touched me?" Jesus knew with whom he was dealing
And the trembling woman saw her healing as stealing.
She fell at Jesus' feet and confessed to what she had done.
"Daughter, your faith has made you well." Her victory won!

And the grave curse of her appalling blood affliction
Was healed, too, with her lost spiritual condition.
And, oh, how grateful we should be
That Jesus' love saved you and me!

(Mark 5:25-34)

NICODEMUS

Israel's esteemed preeminent teacher
Sought out the cosmos' supreme preacher.
Nicodemus came searching for Jesus by night,
Curious to learn and gain spiritual light.

Fanatically religious, but no closer to heaven
Than a loaf of bread with a pinch of leaven.
And even though he came with a desire to learn,
Clueless, his sinful heart must be overturned.

Because of Jesus' miracles, Nicodemus now believes,
But not that saving faith on which the Spirit breathes.
Believing that good works earn your salvation
Is denying that intimate, godly relation.

When Jesus said, "You must be born again,"
Nicodemus was jarred to his core and hardly could stand.
He understood symbolism and was not naïve,
But what he heard he simply could not believe!

If true, his own beliefs were but a façade
Of all he had learned and believed about God.
His pharisaical righteousness and biblical illiteracy
Were contrasting and contradictory to Jesus' true ministry.

Nicodemus from the Old Testament ought to have known
Salvation is by grace through faith alone.
The bronze serpent and Moses, Jesus patiently reminded,
And marveled that Nicodemus had been so blinded.

Upon hearing that Jesus loved the world, not just the Jews,
His ego was shattered with this unthinkable news.
Flailing and writhing under Jesus' loving assault,
Knowing not with Jesus' blood he had been bought.

So, stunned, he simply walked silently away,
But the seed Jesus planted bore fruit one day.
Nicodemus encouraged the Pharisees to keep their own laws,
But they viciously denounced him without just cause.

When Jesus died and hung still on the cross,
His followers despaired, all hope was lost.
But the Sabbath was coming and no time to waste;
Jesus' body must be tended, and that with great haste.

Pilate gave Joseph permission to take Jesus down,
And Nicodemus was waiting there, just to be found.
Joseph's and Nicodemus' hearts, once darkened with vices,
Humbly and lovingly wrapped Jesus' body with spices.

Oh, to be there on that dark, dismal day;
In that cold, rock-hewn tomb where their Master lay.
But soon He would burst forth from His unlawful demise,
And hundreds would see Jesus — with their very own eyes!

(John 19:38-42)

Jesus Cures a Paralyzed Servant

In Capernaum, Jesus went about doing good
To all who asked him or truly believed He could.
A Roman centurion came begging for Jesus' favor;
A military officer, whose strong faith did not waver.

This centurion came to Jesus with a soulful request.
Not from his servant begging him, but at his own behest.
For in his abode, his valued servant lay tormented and paralyzed,
And the centurion's heart was broken, for his servant he greatly prized.

It was readily known that, for this paralytic condition,
There was hardly a cure for this dreadfully dire affliction.
But this Gentile believer, in his anguish and grief,
Held firm in his spirit to his burning belief.

"I will go and heal your servant," Jesus said,
But he knew Jesus need not stand beside his servant's bed.
For as a centurion, he could order soldiers from a distance,
And they would promptly obey without cause for resistance.

"Lord, I do not deserve that you come under my roof."
And Jesus saw that his anchored belief needed no proof,
And beheld the caring heart that pulsed within his breast;
The humility and self-abasement that none could have guessed.

The officer spoke, "Your power, here and now, can make his sickness go,
And end my servant's nightmare of agony and fear and woe."
Jesus stood amazed! "I have not seen any man
"With such trusting faith throughout this land!"

Yes, and many consecrated Gentiles will enter into heaven's glory
And sit down with Abraham, Isaac and Jacob, and hear their sacred story.
While many an Israelite, so religious and pious, will go —
Without a change of heart to the ghastly pit below.

"Go on home, it is as you believed," Jesus said.
"Your servant is sound and has risen from his bed."
And the centurion learned that at the exact hour,
His sick servant was healed by Jesus' awesome power.

If we will only stretch our hearts to believe,
Our expectant faith will most surely conceive.
For there is no lack in our Almighty King,
But only lack of faith in us ...

For He can do anything!

(Matthew 8:5-13)

JESUS WALKS ON WATER

In their boat, Jesus sent the disciples away,
While He went up the mountain alone to pray.
Jesus prayed till the fourth watch of the night,
Yet still the darkness hid the light.

The disciples were in the boat far from land.
The voyage was fair at first, but now they need a saving hand.
For suddenly the night turned ferociously stormy, surprising them there,
While the Lord labored in deep and zealous prayer.

In the beginning the disciples felt little doubt,
Because Jesus is the one who sent them out.
They sailed forward in the storm, changing not their tack.
The disciples trusted Jesus and did not dare turn back.

But now the violent wind and waves convulsed the boat.
The men were wildly fearful that they could not stay afloat.
Why had Jesus sent them into the storm,
To panic them and leave them there forlorn?

Jesus stepped out, the waves humbled themselves at His feet;
And Jesus glowed as He walked serenely across the deep.
The terrified disciples thought Him an apparition,
But it was the Lord Jesus on His saving mission.

The disciples screamed in dreadful fear,
Not remembering the gracious Lord walks ever near.
Claiming to have faith, we must first be tested
To recognize the One in whom our faith is invested.

Sometimes we allow our hearts to be shattered to dust,
When Jesus is standing right there beside us.
Jesus, in compassion, spoke, "Don't be afraid. It is I."
Now their fear rested when Jesus drew nigh.

Peter spoke, "If it is you, Lord, tell me to come walking on the water."
Jesus said, "Come." Peter stepped out gingerly but did not loiter.
Peter wisely waited for an invitation,
For dangerous ventures truly need confirmation.

So courageous Peter walked miraculously upon the lake,
But the roaring winds his courage did forsake.
"Save me, Lord," the now-sinking Peter shouted
As his courage failed and himself he now fully doubted.

Peter, at first, had bold faith and zeal,
And walked upon the water until
He forsook Jesus' face and focused on the howling wind.
And now had only himself on whom to depend.

Jesus reached out and caught him
As He does with us when hope grows dim.
"Oh, you of little faith. Why did you doubt?
"Have I not taught you what faith is all about?"

Into the boat, Jesus and Peter climbed;
The disciples now perceived Jesus supremely exalted and divine.
The winds on the lake and in their hearts did cease,
And there fell upon them a heavenly, euphoric peace.

They joyfully gave Jesus the adoration due Him,
For now they believed they really knew Him.
Worshipping and exclaiming,
"Truly, You are the Son of God!"

(Matthew 14:22-33)

The Canaanite Woman

To Jesus the woman made her confession;
Her daughter was under demonic possession.
And the woman's heart was broken and bleeding;
A touch from Jesus was all she was needing.

"Lord, Son of David, have mercy on me!"
Not merit, but mercy, she knew held the key.
Jesus answers the woman not a single word.
He turned a deaf ear as if He had not heard.

Oh! How discouraged she must have felt,
A silence of pain Jesus had dealt.
But every prayer is not answered immediately,
And often must be prayed for repeatedly.

The disciples wanted Jesus to answer her prayer,
But since He did not, they ceased to care.
"Send her away; she makes such a fuss.
Stop her from following after us!"

Jesus said, "I was sent only to Israel's lost sheep."
The woman was broken and began to weep.
It was a repulse and reproach Jesus gave!
She staggered under His words so grave.

But she worshipped Jesus and cried, "Sir, help me!
Please don't leave and then forget me."
"Bread for the children must not be fed to the dogs," Jesus said.
And with that, she stood and lifted her head.

To Jesus' hard word, she grew perplexed and mindless
And did not respond to His seeming unkindness.
Feeling that her hope now was dim,
She blames herself instead of Him.

"But even the puppies," said she, "eat the crumbs that fall,
And they are not grudged the crumbs at all!"
Faith finds encouragement even in loss,
And hangs on tightly whatever the cost.

This woman showed wisdom, patience and meekness,
Which overcame her heartbreak, fear and weakness.
But of all the graces, faith honors Christ most,
A work in a humble heart by the Holy Ghost.

"Woman, you have great faith," Jesus said.
Oh! How her soul rose up from the dead!
His words were like rain on a sun-parched earth,
And her heart exploded with rejoicing and mirth!

Jesus wanted her faith to prove,
And to a higher level her faith to move.
"Your request is granted." Her race was run.
He spoke, and it was immediately done!

A Canaanite woman, so lost and miserable,
Proved herself a true daughter of Israel!
We, too, have no merit on which to depend;
God's awesome grace only has grafted us in.

(Matthew 15:21-28)

Jesus Ousts an Evil Spirit

In Capernaum, Jesus on the Sabbath day
Went to the synagogue there to convey
His doctrine of salvation, mercy and peace,
And from Satan's dread hold their lives to release.

As Jesus expounded His profound godly preaching,
The astonished people marveled at this new teaching.
With authority Jesus taught the law, a school master,
And how the self-righteous pave their road to disaster.

"What do you want with us?" a foul spirit abruptly screamed.
"You, the Holy One of God: we the lost, the unredeemed.
"Jesus of Nazareth, we know who you are and know your power.
"Have you come to destroy us?" he smirked with a cower.

"Be muzzled! Come out of him!" Jesus said to him sternly.
The filthy spirit obeyed but still held the man firmly,
And shook him violently, raging with a shriek;
But the man was not hurt, though trembling and weak.

"Even evil spirits submit to him!" the people cried;
That this Holy One came forth from God cannot be denied!
They were, one and all, thunderstruck in miraculous surprise
As they beheld Jesus' miracle with their very own eyes.

How pitiful for evil spirits as soon as tomorrow
Will burn in cruel flames forever in horror.
Oh, how thankful and humbled we should be
That the gracious Lord Jesus chose you and me.

In that bright celestial city, no more sin, no more curse,
While our blissful, glorious songs to God array the universe.
Let our hearts burst forth in praise whenever then we meet
And dream of casting our golden crowns at Jesus' precious feet!

(Luke 4:31-37)

THE TEN LEPERS

In solitude, Jesus walked the dusty way
Toward a little village where He planned to stay.
He was quite weary but took no care
For He knew He had a mission there.

Calling out to Jesus were ten leprous men;
Many presumed them racked by sin.
The Jews thought lepers mirrored God's displeasure;
But God saw them as an opportune treasure.

Loudly, they called, "Jesus, Master, have pity on us!"
Not asking for healing, but for what Jesus thought just.
In respect, the nine lepers were precisely the bottom,
Yet the Samaritan was lower as if from Sodom.

"Go show yourself to the priest," Jesus said,
And in going they were healed from their toes to their head.
Yet only one returned, praising God loudly,
Giving himself to Jesus both humbly and proudly.

All his love to his Lord to greet
Throwing himself at Jesus' feet.
The nine were healed by Jesus' compassion and power;
But the Samaritan, by faith, being saved that hour!

(Luke 17:11-19)

The Memorial Gift

Simon, the healed leper, was the host,
Invited Martha, the homemaker, who knew the most
About making guests comfortable and at ease,
Cooking and serving with a kind heart to please.

And Jesus sat there with Lazarus beside Him,
Another sat there who soon would deny Him.
And Mary was there, who had once taken a seat
And chose the best part at Jesus' sweet feet.

Mary remembered the woman sinner
Who poured out the perfume on Jesus at dinner;
And how Jesus forgave her of all her sin
And sent her in peace a new life to begin.

Now Mary was given prophetic understanding
Of Jesus' soon coming death at God's commanding.
A pound of precious spikenard in an alabaster box,
She had kept it safe under key and lock.

So Mary broke open the box, spilling its contents,
The indignant disciples thought it foolish nonsense.
When she poured out the costly perfume on Jesus' feet and head,
They thought surely it should have been sold instead.

The disciples were thoughtless and needed teaching
But they truly loved Jesus and had grown from His preaching.
And they had repented and given their hearts to Him,
Even though their understanding was often quite dim.

But Judas Iscariot was the one most let down
And his face convulsed in an acid frown;
For his greedy heart was as black as his beard,
It was loss of the money for the bag he feared.

Anointing Jesus for His burial was Mary's holy purpose;
The sweet smell so costly as she poured out the surplus.
And seeing that Jesus was so graciously pleased,
The disciples by their consciences now were seized.

Jesus was so gratified, He made it no mystery
That Mary's love gift would be remembered through history.
"The poor you will have with you always,
But I will be with you just a few more days."

Is the hoard in your alabaster box "just mine alone"?
Friend, who then is sitting upon the throne?
Remember, when on earth or to glorious heaven you've gone
God will reward abundantly those loving gifts you have sown.

(John 12:1-9; Matthew 26:6-13)

Jesus Heals Blind Eyes

A blind man from birth who had suffered so long
Led the disciples to ask Jesus who had done wrong.
Jesus answered, "Neither this man nor his parents sinned,
But to show God's power — a new life to begin!"

Jesus spat on the ground and made mud with His spittle,
And those watching thought it a ridiculous riddle.
Jesus spread the mud over the eyes of the man
And quickly to the pool of Siloam he ran!

When he cleansed his eyes from the dirt and spittle,
No longer was it a ridiculous riddle.
For light poured in and illuminated the beggar's eyes,
No logic, reason or reckoning justified.

The beggar was ecstatic and felt so blessed.
"It was that good man," he gladly confessed.
The beggar just glowed with eyes so bright,
One might think he could light up the night!

The Jews demanded, "Is that the same fellow — that beggar man?
"The one who has always the outstretched hand?"
"I am the same man," the beggar bravely replied.
Many confirmed his truth, but some denied.

The Pharisees hassled the beggar on how he could see;
"I'll tell you the truth if only you'll listen to me.
"That man put mud on my eyes and sent me to Siloam to wash them out
"And here's my honest report: I can see clearly, and that without doubt."

They hounded the beggar once again, "What did He do?"
"Surely, of all people, you must know how he healed you."
"I told you once," the beggar said, "but you would not hear.
"Why are you so stubborn; what do you have to fear?"

"We are disciples of Moses," they reviled, "to whom God did speak.
"That fellow speaks to rabble, the ignorant and every common freak!"
They found taunting the beggar so fulfillingly delicious,
Their hearts were further hardened and became even more vicious.

Not to be bullied, the beggar countered, "Why this is a very curious thing!
"He healed my blindness, and you don't even know His name!
"Since time began, nobody has opened the eyes of the blind:
"That man was a prophet from God, noble and kind."

So bloated with religious education,
Smug in their robes of self-adulation,
They missed the glorious miracle of the beggar's sight,
Willfully blind, preferring darkness to light.

Livid with rage, the Pharisees queried his mother and father,
Which was more sinister than a worrisome bother.
For the Pharisees had power to bar members from the synagogue,
Drowning their life in darkness as surely as a bog.

The parents feared that their celebration
Could quickly turn into excommunication.
For it was unquestionable that the Jewish leaders' desire
Was to oust any believer in Jesus as the Messiah.

If expelled, the parents would be total outcasts,
Utterly hopeless, for a lifetime it would last.
They would never be able to buy or sell,
Nor be remembered or honored by a funeral.

The officials angrily challenged the parents, "Was your son born blind?"
And his parents understood their intent to malign.
"Yes, he was born blind, but we don't know more;
"Except for his sight, he's the same as before."

The Pharisees claimed that Jesus was a sinner.
Their hearts, without wisdom, were as cold as the winter.
They thought it a crime that Jesus healed on the Sabbath day;
And from their loathing, they wanted Jesus' blood for pay.

The Jewish leaders continued baiting the beggar with constant quiz:
"The man who opened your eyes — who do you say He is?"
"I told you he must be a prophet sent from God," he replied,
But they stubbornly held to their unbelief and that he had lied.

"Give glory to God," they foamed, "for Jesus is an evil person."
Disagreeing with them, the beggar knew, his life might worsen.
"Good or bad, I don't know, but I was blind and now I see!
"And this, too, I know: Jesus is the one who healed me!"

The Pharisees began to jeer and curse:
"You illegitimate bastard, you! Of all people, you're the worst!"
At the synagogue they thrilled to expunge his name, making him an outcast.
Many were gleeful, while others were puzzled or wholly aghast.

Jesus returned and asked, "Do you believe in the Messiah?"
The trembling beggar asked, "Who is He, sir, for I want to!"
"You have seen Him," Jesus said, "and He is speaking to you."
"Yes, Lord, I believe!" and he praised and worshiped Him, too.

Oh, how despairing for those who listen to God's Word
And on listening have not truly heard.
They cannot enter through God's heavenly gate;
For the self-righteous, it will be always too late.

But for this poor, humble beggar from eternity ordained
Faithed on Jesus and believed on His name.
God gifted him blindness, and he was not to blame,
For the miracle brought great glory to God's holy name.

The boastful and prideful Pharisees
Ought to have been humbled to their knees.
Their hearts had hardened into non-porous rock
And their shriveled souls could only mock.

But let us carefully search our own hearts
And make certain there are no wayward parts.
Let us humble ourselves through prayer.
And ask forgiveness for any pride lurking there.

(John 9:1-41)

Who Is My Neighbor?

An expert in the law came asking Jesus a question.
Jesus expressed truths that should have brought confession.
But as to loving God, the expert would say no more,
As to loving his neighbor, he believed his a perfect score.

When the expert said, "You shall love your neighbor," he barred Gentiles.
Now Jesus must correct his prejudice and end his faulty wiles.
So He tells the man a parable of a Samaritan and a Jew,
And if he listens carefully, he will find out what he ought to want to do.

A certain businessman traveled down the Jericho Road,
With valuable merchandise in his purse, but not a heavy load.
Then thieves stole his precious goods and beat him 'til half dead,
And left him with bloody wounds upon his limbs and face and head.

Fortunately, the heavens opened and there came a godly priest,
However, he was running late for a celebratory feast.
By the victim's cries and moans, he felt genuinely appalled,
But, regrettably, to this grand event he had first been called.

By God's grace, there came a pious and zealous Levite,
Angered by the victim's wounds, he deeply felt his plight.
And by this heinous deed, he was so offended
That he prayed briefly, but his plans could not be upended.

With utter compassion these two meant quite well.
The priest wanted justice and heaven heard him rail.
The sensitive Levite could not bear the sight of blood at all,
But both were sure someone else would answer his desperate call.

Then there came a despised Samaritan down the road;
His first thought to get the victim to a safe abode.
And his pity takes on a supernatural life of its own,
When he sees the poor man's bleeding and hears his woeful groan.

Washing and soothing the wounds with oil and wine,
He prayed for his healing to the One merciful and divine.
He bandaged his wounds from his own linen,
And prayed for those who had been abusive and sinning.

With the patient on his donkey, he walked along slowly
And in his spirit clearly heard the angels singing lowly.
And with kindness and compassion he took him to an inn
And paid two coins to the innkeeper on whom he could depend.

With tender words of encouragement, he bedded the man down
And promised to pay the extra cost the next time he came around.
And on his knees, he prayed for the man's healing and for the situation
That led to the privilege of helping and his heartfelt jubilation.

We were like that traveler, walking in spiritual death,
When Jesus, that good Samaritan, brought salvation's saving breath.
Are we like that expert who, behind his question, hid?
Or are we like the Samaritan and the loving good he did?

(Luke 10:25-37)

What the Samaritan gave:
— eyes
— heart
— beast
— feet
— hands
— time
— money

What the Samaritan did:
— touched
— washed
— bandaged
— took to safe place
— prayed
— encouraged
— bedded him down

Jesus Heals a Shriveled Hand

Jesus walked into the synagogue and stood,
Seeking opportunities to serve and to do good.
Another stood there with a shriveled hand,
Not able to do what others can.

The Pharisees cared not for this disabled man,
Unable to earn a living with his useless hand.
The spectators there were so harshly unkind
And the Physician and patient were both maligned.

The pitiful man came there looking for kindness,
But found painful rejection and intentional blindness.
Why wouldn't they want to help their neighbor
And be zealous for Jesus' miracle favor?

But if Jesus dared show Himself a miracle maker,
They threatened to charge him as a Sabbath breaker.
Jesus gave them an opportunity to feel the man's plight,
Which would lead to compassion and set their hearts right.

"Which is lawful on the Sabbath: to do good or evil?
"Whether is better: to save life or kill?"
A question that contained the answer so clear
They answered not, less they lose their veneer.

Their stubbornness a high wall blocking them in
And sealing them off in their cold tomb of sin.
Jesus was sorely distressed at their being so spiritually dumb,
For how lovingly He had called them, but they refused to come.

Jesus said to the man, "Stretch out your hand."
And the man immediately obeyed Jesus' command.
His hand, by Jesus' power, now made strong and whole,
And how he praised Jesus with all his heart and soul!

Our hands, a great marvel of God's awesome creation,
Embrace talents and gifts within our church congregation.
So fold your hands in secret prayer —
And praise God for the miracles shrouded there!

(Matthew 9:32-34)

Jarius' Daughter Raised

As Jesus was talking, Jarius came
Fully believing in Jesus' name.
A man of honor and highly esteemed,
A man of all virtues it truly seemed.

His little girl lay at death's door,
And he hardly wanted to live anymore.
A grief that pierced like a wooden stake
In his heart for the child that death might take.

And his heart bled from the stabbing pain,
Yet trusting solely in Jesus' name.
Pleading desperately with longing so deep,
Throwing himself humbly at Jesus' feet.

"Please come and touch her, and she will revive,
"For you, Jesus only, can raise her alive."
This winsome child so dear to his heart,
The loss of her would tear him apart.

He remembered her now, how curls framed her small face
And her dark eyes were pools of beauty and grace.
He had often seen her feeding the birds
And heard her sweet singing as she made up the words.

She picked the flowers that grew by the way
And bestowed them graciously, denying her play.
The forest animals would eat from her hand
And go back to their dens at her command.

Oh, what a blessing to family and neighbors,
The love she spent with her kind little favors.
God seemed to have given her a special light
As she prayed for others day and night.

Suddenly, sad words howled through death's dark door;
The messengers wailed, "Why bother the Teacher anymore?"
Jarius' heart sank in a pit of gloom
And his mind's eye saw her cold in the tomb.

Jesus said, "Don't be afraid, just trust Me.
"She's only there sleeping, as you will see."
So Jarius' faith stood up boldly and without a doubt
Believed one touch from Jesus, death would spit the child out!

The relations and friends were wretched with grief,
And the kind words of comfort brought no relief.
For they all laughed scornfully when Jesus said,
"The child only sleeps and is not really dead."

This company of people whom death made cower
Were so ignorant of Jesus' mighty power.
Their hearts were muddled, hardened and cold,
For unbelief had taken a staggering toll.

Jesus took His disciples and her parents to where she was lying,
To the room where the throng had seen the child dying.
Jesus took her hand and said, "Get up, little girl."
And this miracle was proclaimed throughout the whole world.

The damsel thanked Jesus with a smile so wide.
That she had been dead could not be denied.
Her parents delirious with joy for such grace
Could not take their eyes from her shining face.

Dear friend, if you, too, would have a new life
Freed from your fears, bitterness and strife;
Just ask the Savior to come into your heart,
Forgive all your sins and gain a new start.

(Mark 5:21-24, 35-43)

The Crown of Thorns

Jesus wore the crown for me,
The crown of thorns that set me free.
The weight of sin upon His breast
Brought precious peace and perfect rest.

A crown of long, sharp thorns was made,
Upon the Savior's head was laid.
Deformed hearts with twisted bent
Could not bear the innocent.

Soldiers stripped off the clothes He wore;
They gawked and laughed and plotted more.
A purple robe on Him was laid;
In ignorance, Jesus' divinity, displayed.

With reed, they smote that sacred head,
Stumbling and staggering He freely bled.
Mocking Jesus, they bowed the knee,
Hailed Him with Satanic glee.

While thorns pierced His scalp and cheek,
The Lord submitted bowed and meek.
Blood and sweat mingled down,
While trembling angels hovered 'round.

They struck with fists and slapped with palm;
No hope for Him, no heaven's balm.
Soldiers reveled, and with joy they looked
At the fiendish blows our Master took.

They spat on Him with putrid breath,
Excited by His coming death.
Tears of forgiveness flowed down His face,
Without one soul to plead His case.

Jesus wore the crown for me,
The crown of thorns that set us free.
What did we sinners receive instead?
A crown of glory for our head! (Psalm 8:5)

I ask you, friend, if you were there,
Would you be one to jeer or stare?
Perhaps you believe down in your heart
That you would not have taken part.

But if you claim you truly care,
You know that you were really there.

(Matthew, Mark, Luke and John)

Jesus Amazes the Scholars

Many there came up to the Passover Feast,
Those most faithful and those who were least.
The caravan was alive with deep conversation and laughter,
Of the past and the now and the coming hereafter.

Twelve-year-old Jesus and His parents were part of this throng,
Never imagining that things might go terribly wrong.
Mary and Joseph stayed til the end of the ordinance,
Worshiping and praising, sharing in replete accordance.

But on their return to Nazareth, Jesus could not be found.
Though they searched diligently, He was simply nowhere around.
Very distraught, the parents traveled hurriedly back to the city,
And Joseph comforted Mary, who blamed herself without pity.

They had sought among family, neighbors and friends,
And saw in their spirits the devil's sly grins.
And, oh, the heartache, the confusion and gnawing pain,
Their self-reproach as parents dealt a dark, ugly stain.

And just when they were about to despair,
They found Jesus in the Temple there!
And it seemed a soft glow illumined His face,
And His words were deep wells of wisdom and grace.

They so wondered and marveled greatly at what they saw;
He was seated, not standing, with the teachers of the law.
They were amazed at the respect He was given and received,
And their hearts bubbled over and their minds now relieved.

But Mary sweetly and privately admonished Him,
For her understanding was troubled, puzzled and dim.
"Did you not know I must be in my father's house?" Jesus revealed,
And Mary hid His words deep in her heart — and there they were sealed.

Oh, that we, too, might give Jesus a seat within our hearts;
Give our lives to Him, with all the wayward parts.
And if we have lost Jesus, like His parents, we must dare —
To go back to where we lost Him, and find Him waiting there!

(Luke 2:41-51)

Jesus Heals a Leper

Many there came to hear Jesus speak,
The proud, the rebellious, a few who were meek.
Many hearts were much amazed,
But few hearts were set ablaze.

For most hearts were dark or dim
Without godly desire to cling to Him.
But a small remnant came in humble participation,
Returning Jesus' love with heartfelt adoration.

Some saw leprosy as from the hand of God
That struck evil with power, like the shepherd's rod.
Never thinking that Jesus' hand
Could cure a leper or any man.

And never thinking any higher,
Unable to imagine Jesus as Messiah.
But the leper came with healthy lust,
Knelt before Jesus sincerely with trust.

"Lord, if You are willing, You can make me clean."
Assured of Jesus' power, a faith not often seen.
And with a humble submission to Jesus' will,
No matter what Jesus' answer, he would love Him still.

Jesus reached out and touched the loathsome limb.
"I am willing, be clean," Jesus spoke to him.
And immediately the joyful leper was cured,
Losing memory of the horror he had so long endured.

Jesus healing him was not in stone set,
But issued from a humble request that Jesus gladly met.
And Jesus said He would,
Because the leper believed He could!

A few seeing the miracle were now convinced,
Jesus heals immediately without recompense.
And Jesus heals our sin, the leprosy of the soul;
Sin corrupts completely and takes a devastating toll.

Jesus lovingly commanded,
"Don't tell anyone.
And go show yourself to the priest;
And offer the gift Moses commanded."

Jesus wanted him to be seen,
So the priest could declare him completely clean.
Are we completely clean? We must do our part
And allow Jesus, our High Priest, to look into *our* heart.

(Matthew 8:1-4)

OTHER CONTEMPLATIONS

THE ROSE OF SHARON

In a world so cold and barren
Grew the red-red Rose of Sharon.
From a root in dry ground springing,
Hope and joy, Salvation bringing.

The crimson Rose through heaven's gate
Provoked deep love or bitter hate.
The reddest rose on sin-lost earth
Came to give life, the second birth.

Healing diseases of every kind;
Brought new life to the deaf and blind.
Spoke a lame man from his bed;
Awakened Lazarus from the dead.

And for these marvelous, wondrous deeds,
There grew hatred, jealousy, demonic weeds.
Hideous tongues, horrid and spiteful,
Spewed vicious words vile and frightful.

Then the holy Rose was cruelly crushed
And from torn petals the red-red gushed.
Many there were who railed and scorned,
But few there were who wailed and mourned.

So with mighty power, God's grand design
Swept death to his dungeon, a prophetic sign.
The Rose of Sharon, blossomed once more
In splendid array as never before.

The Rose of Sharon, the awesome sacrifice,
Paid for our sins the ultimate price.
None other than God's own son,
Our Lord and Savior — JESUS CHRIST.

Rachel and Leah

When Rachel had no children,
And Leah had no love,
Rachel went to Jacob,
Leah to God above.

And because Leah was unloved,
Some thought it unscientific,
That somehow she did manage
To become somewhat prolific.

Leah boasted of her four children:
Reuben, Simeon, Levi and Judah.
And Rachel became quite jealous
When Leah would toot her tooter.

So Rachel went to Jacob,
"Give me children or I die!"
"Don't get mad at me," said he,
"God's in charge, NOT I!"

So Rachel gave him Bilhah;
Jacob was happy as could be.
And when he saw his baby Dan,
Said, "Wow, he looks so much like me!"

Now Bilhah made Rachel jealous.
She said, "Jacob, stop this dally!"
But her warning came too late,
For out popped lil' Naphtali.

But this unsettled Leah,
Truly a competitive dame.
So she gave Jacob Zilpah,
"We, too, can play that game!"

So after the game was over,
There appeared this one named Gad.
Jacob and Zilpah were happy,
But it just made Rachel mad!

Again, with Zilpah the game was played
And Rachel made a jealous dash
When she saw Leah's tiny newborn,
The pair had nicknamed him Ash.

So Leah bought her husband,
And love apples were the price.
She gave birth to baby Issachar,
But still not a happy wife.

Though unloved, Leah had another son,
Jacob's honor she hoped to earn.
When Rachel saw Zeb, their precious new one,
She stomped out the door with a jealous heartburn.

At last, Leah got her druthers,
Little Dinah made happiness abound;
For now her older brothers
Had a sister to kick around.

Then God remembered Rachel's plight;
Jacob gladly did comply.
And to them a handsome son was born —
Joseph, the apple of Jacob's eye.

Then Rachel bore another son.
Said she, "Benjamin's from Jehovah!"
Then Jacob, at last, had a chance to speak.
Said he, "I think my game is over!"

Now if your family's a muddle, dear,
Ungracious, rude and unpunctual,
Just remember Rachel and Leah,
Whose home was truly dysfunctional.

Even so, Joseph, Rachel's son, saved many lives
And what an example of how to live!
Had one, not several, wives
And taught his brothers to forgive.

From Judah's lineage, Leah's son,
Came the most prophetic one.
He paid the most exorbitant price,
To forgive our sins and make us right.

None other than
Our Lord and Savior, Jesus Christ!

And if your family is truly a mess,
Just go to Jesus and truly confess.
He will transform your home,
Make it sweeter than the honeycomb,
And give you the needed rest.

(Genesis 29 and 30)

A Greater Thing

Glorious and good is our God,
Mighty and merciful is He;
He wings across the mountaintops
And walks upon the sea.

He scatters glittering jewels by night,
Guides the burning ball by day;
Hurls lightning bolts that crack the night,
That gives me pause to pray.

He churns the ocean's seething tide,
Its fragrance deep and wild;
He awakens the grumbling volcano's blast,
Then thunders through the mountain pass,
While hailstones rain on stormy heights
Unveils the moon to awe the night.

Yet a greater thing than these He's done —
Hallelujah! Praise God! He gave us His Son!

David and Abigail

In the wilderness of Paran near Carmel Village,
The wealthy ranch owner, Nabal, owned sheep, goats and tillage.
He was exuberant in luxury, cheap in charity,
Noted was he for his vile rascality.

While in the wilderness, David's men offered a protective arm
For Nabal's sheep and goats and kept them from all harm.
Killing wild animals that could have raided the flock,
And with roving bands they did with swiftness block.

David sent ten hungry men with a modest petition,
For their needs were real and not just foolish fiction.
David's message to Nabal was as from a servant or son,
Not boasting about all the good for him they had done.

But surly Nabal denied and abused David's men,
Hurling insults despite how respectful they had been.
Hearing this, David's righteous anger was overcome;
As explosive rage seized him, striking him spiritually dumb.

"God curse me if one of his men remains alive!"
We will sting with vengeance like bees from a hive,
And by Satan, David was set on fire of hell.
No words his horrid temper could mend or veil.

This ragtag crew idolized David with an avowed bloody loyalty;
Dedicated to his protection, vastly esteeming his God-appointed royalty.
David furiously strapped on his sword with strength he had not known,
Revenge circulated through his heart and into his very bone.

Plundering time, David and his men thundered through the land,
With murder in their hearts and judgment in their hand.
As David slowed their pace descending a hill,
An image appeared, and though winded, made his heart stand still.

But Abigail's lovely face was but a firefly's glow to her spirit;
Her gracious, generous self, framed her lifelong lyric.
From her servants, she knew that David was understandably irate;
And death was surely the price with no debate.

Other words cannot tell of Abigail's magnificent appeal,
If one is humble, it will truly any marriage heal.
Dear Sister, read of how she made her humble plea
And pray God will grant her wisdom to you and me.

Abigail dismounted her donkey and humbly bowed low,
Wisdom is better than weapons, she wanted David to know.
For all the love on earth, all love is despite,
And she loved Nabal with compassion and godly insight.

"My Lord, let the blame be on me alone,"
And there rose up in her spirit a deep and heavy groan.
Abigail speaks passionately to David with deference and respect;
And with prudent, charming speech, she atones for Nabal's neglect.

"My husband is a selfish fool," Abigail said,
"But I am at your service to see that you're well fed.
Here's bread and roasted grain and choice cakes of raisins, too,
Wine and sweet cakes of figs all for your men and you."

"Bless the Lord God of Israel," David responded to Abigail,
"For without you, there would not have been left one male.
And if I had taken that evil dolt's life
The matter would have ended in bitterness and strife."

"Thank God for your goodly common sense,
And your gifted tongue to tame and convince."
David accepted the excellent provisions proffered;
"I will not kill your husband; go home without fear," he offered.

When Nabal, the next day, heard what had taken place,
He had a fatal stroke, collapsing forward, falling on his face.
What a miserable man with an evil-loving bent
And a devil's heart of stone that refused to repent.

When David heard that Nabal was dead,
He felt no sorrow, but praised God for justice instead.
Smitten first by Abigail's beauty, then by her God-fearing life,
David sent messengers to ask Abigail to become his wife.

In great modesty, Abigail yielded to David's request,
Knowing that David had no crown or throne as yet.
But Abigail was so moved by his teachable humility,
And into her heart, there flowed a joyful tranquility.

Quickly she prepared for the journey to meet her king,
Hardly considering she was moving from much to barely anything.
On her donkey and with her five maidens, she followed David's crew,
And with each step they took, her love for David grew.

The wilderness wind swept softly through the trees
As they rode along,
And the maidens sang of David's exploits and feats
In jubilant, glorious song.

Then David appeared,
And Abigail's heart was drained of sorrow
As he gathered her in his arms,
Embracing her with precious promises for tomorrow.

(1 Samuel 25:1-42)

Prayer/Thoughts for Israel

O how God loves Jerusalem,
the sacred city,
the navel of the earth,
The apple of God's eye.

God has chosen His people from all the peoples of the earth,
Not for anything they have done —
But because He, He Himself, has set his love upon them.

Like a mother tending a wayward child,
He has drawn them back time and time again to Himself,
Sometimes allowing them to experience the pain of their rebellion
because of His overwhelming love.

May the enemies of Israel perish!
May the hatred in their hearts and the weapons in their hands
Boomerang a Davidic vengeance upon them.
May the enemies' rockets veer wild in the wilderness,
Sparing even the meanest shrub and the least of the forest creatures.

May the fear of the children be as flint to their bones;
And may they grow, mature and proliferate
as their forefathers in the wilderness.

May hunger flee to the hills and pain perish in the beloved sea.
May emigres soar safely to their new homes on wings of eagles,
their Aliyah another fulfillment of prophecy.

May the desert bloom
with blinding and riotous colors:
Gauntlet greens, defiant reds —
Screaming out the blessings of God
Upon Holy Israel
To the surrounding jealous nations.

And may God dance in delight
Over His people;
And ring out an eternal reverberating blessing
Upon each chosen one.

Selah.

Plan of Salvation

How to Become a Christian

Do you wish to accept the gift of eternal life that Jesus is offering you?

Let's look at what this commitment involves:

- I acknowledge I am a sinner in need of a Savior; this is to repent or turn away from sin.
- I believe in my heart that God raised Jesus from the dead; this is to trust that Jesus paid the full penalty for my sins.
- I confess Jesus as my Lord and my God; this is to surrender control of my life to Jesus.
- I receive Jesus as my Savior forever; this is to accept that God has done for me, and in me, what He promised.

If it is your sincere desire to receive Jesus into your heart as your personal Lord and Savior, then talk to God from your heart. Here's a suggested prayer:

Lord Jesus, I know that I am a sinner and I do not deserve eternal life. But I believe You died and rose from the grave to make me a new creation and to prepare me to dwell in your presence forever. Jesus, come into my life, take control of my life, forgive my sins and save me. I am now placing my trust in You alone for my salvation and I accept your free gift of eternal life.

If you have trusted Jesus as your Lord and Savior, tell others, and join the fellowship of a local church. Other believers want to rejoice in what God has done in your life and help you to grow spiritually.

(From "How to Become a Christian," at SBC.net)

www.ingramcontent.com/pod-product-compliance
Lightning Source LLC
Chambersburg PA
CBHW070654050426
42451CB00008B/348